The Art of Office Combat: Conquer Your Workplace, One Disaster at a Time

Marako Marcus

Published by Marako Marcus, 2024.

Copyright Page

While every precaution has been taken in the preparation of this book, the publisher assumes no responsibility for errors or omissions, or for damages resulting from the use of the information contained herein. No part of this book may be reproduced, stored in a retrieval system, or transmitted in any form or by any means, electronic, mechanical, photocopying, recording, or otherwise, without the prior written permission of the publisher, except as permitted by applicable copyright law. The information and views expressed in this book are those of the author and do not necessarily reflect the views of any organization or entity. All names, characters, and incidents in this book are fictitious. Any resemblance to real persons, living or dead, is purely coincidental.

The Art of Office Combat: Conquer Your Workplace, One Disaster at a Time

First Edition, December 18, 2024.

Copyright © 2024 Marako Marcus.

Written by Marako Marcus.

Welcome to the Battlefield

Congratulations! You've found yourself in the ultimate arena—the office. A place where the coffee is never strong enough, the deadlines are always tight, and the politics are as cutthroat as any battlefield. If you're reading this, chances are you're either stuck in a warzone of passive-aggressive emails, endless meetings, or working for a boss who believes "micromanaging" is a leadership style. But don't worry, you're not alone. Welcome to The Art of Office Combat, where we'll teach you how to fight—and win—in the war of workplace chaos, one disaster at a time.

Let's face it. If you're not battling for survival in your office, you're probably part of the problem. It's a place where the most dangerous weapon isn't a stapler (although, don't discount it), but the sheer incompetence that lurks behind every corner. From the clueless colleague who insists on replying "all" to every email, to the manager who believes "we're a family" but can't remember your name—it's a jungle out there. And the sad truth is, most people don't know how to fight back. They wallow in frustration, gossip in the breakroom, or simply accept the madness as "the way things are."

But here's the deal: It doesn't have to be this way. You can learn to outwit the chaos and come out on top. In this book, we're going to arm you with the tools you need to fight the battles that matter—and win. We'll expose the tactics that make the office a warzone and give you strategies to navigate through the minefield of office politics, incompetence, and apathy.

SO, HOW DO YOU PREPARE for battle? First, understand that you're not going to fight with a sword or a shield, but with your wit, your resilience, and a very sharp sense of humor. When you learn to see the office for what it truly is—a circus of egos, bad ideas, and half-baked strategies—you'll start to fight smarter, not harder. Think of this book as your manual to office warfare, where the ammunition is sarcasm, the strategy is survival, and the goal is to make it out alive, without losing your mind.

We'll explore the key players in this war. The overzealous manager who confuses being a control freak with being "efficient," the coworker who seems to be perpetually absent but still gets credit for your work, and, of course, the organizational dysfunction that lets bad decisions become the norm. And don't get me started on the "company culture" that often feels more like a cult than a workplace.

This is no ordinary self-help book. This is a battle plan, a way to not just survive but thrive in the office battlefield. If you think "toughing it out" and being a passive observer is your only option, think again. We're here to show you how to rise above the nonsense, laugh in the face of office disaster, and get ahead without selling your soul—or your sanity—in the process.

ARE YOU READY TO FIGHT? Let's get started. The war is about to begin.

Chapter 1: The Gossip Mill—How to Navigate the Land of Whispered Lies

Let's talk about the elephant in the room—gossip. It's everywhere in the office, lurking in the corners of the break room, whispered behind cubicle walls, and buzzing around in those "casual" conversations by the water cooler. If you've ever overheard someone say, "I heard from *someone* that..." you've encountered the office gossip mill. And let's face it—this mill runs on drama, misinformation, and sheer nosiness, with a sprinkling of Schadenfreude thrown in for good measure.

Here's the thing: gossip isn't just annoying—it's a silent killer. It erodes trust, spreads rumors, and can make your work life feel like a high school cafeteria where cliques rule and the truth doesn't stand a chance. Imagine this: Sarah from Marketing says, "I heard that Linda from HR is planning to quit, but she's too scared to tell anyone because she's worried about her reputation." Meanwhile, Linda is still sitting there, blissfully unaware, cranking out work like a champ. By the time the rumor reaches you, Linda's "resignation" is already a gossip wildfire that's burned down half the office.

Gossip feeds on insecurities and spreads like wildfire. It's easy for people to jump on the bandwagon, share their own juicy tidbits, and in the process, distort reality into something completely unrecognizable. Take Jason from Finance, for example. He's the office's unofficial "fixer," always "helping" people out of jams. But the rumor mill spins a different story—he's apparently the go-to person for getting "inside info" about what's happening in upper management, and everyone who wants to get ahead is hanging on his every word.

But it's not just about what gets spread—gossip also serves as a smokescreen. It's a way for people to distract themselves from their actual work. If you're not careful, you can find yourself sucked into the drama, responding to emails, or defending yourself over fabricated stories. You may even get blamed for things you didn't do, simply because someone *heard* you did. It's the workplace equivalent of being guilty until proven innocent—and guess what? That's not a fight you want to have.

NOW, HOW DO YOU TACKLE this issue head-on? First, avoid engaging. It's tempting to add your two cents to that juicy office rumor, but trust me—it's not worth it. The more you contribute, the deeper you're sinking into the quicksand. Instead, steer the conversation back to facts or even better, change the subject entirely. "Oh, I haven't heard that one, but what do you think about the upcoming project deadline?"

Next, be the example. If you're in a leadership role or even just a well-respected employee, model the behavior you want to see. When you hear gossip, don't let it fester—address it directly with the person involved. If someone tells you that another colleague is "having issues," your response should be: "You should talk to them directly about it. They're the ones who can give you the full picture."

And when in doubt, shut it down. No, you don't need to give an impassioned speech, but simply saying, "I don't participate in office gossip" will send a strong message. Keep it polite, professional, and short. It works like a charm.

Finally, stay focused. There's a war going on around you—don't get distracted by the noise. If you're in the middle of a project, keep your head down and keep moving forward. Gossip is the office's way of making you lose sight of what actually matters. And remember, those who engage in gossip are usually the ones with the least to offer.

SO, NEXT TIME THE OFFICE gossip mill cranks up, you'll know exactly how to tackle it—head-on, with zero tolerance for nonsense. Stay strong, stay smart, and stay away from the drama.

Chapter 2: The Retaliation Game—How to Handle a Workplace Vendetta

Ah, retaliation—the hidden art of getting even in the workplace. You've probably witnessed it, or worse, been caught in the crossfire. This is the office equivalent of tit-for-tat, but with more passive-aggressive emails and covert sabotage. It's the quiet, underhanded war that can make you feel like you're walking through a minefield, wondering when the next explosion will go off.

Let's break it down. Picture this: you've just finished a meeting where you spoke up about a terrible decision your boss is making. You were polite, respectful, and offered a solution. But now, suddenly, you're on the receiving end of some very cold emails. Your projects are delayed for no apparent reason. Your feedback is ignored. You start to feel like maybe, just maybe, your candid thoughts are starting to come back to haunt you. That's retaliation at work. Subtle, vindictive, and incredibly frustrating.

And it doesn't stop there. Retaliation often comes from colleagues, too. Imagine working with a teammate who's notoriously bad at meeting deadlines. You've had enough, so you point it out in a team meeting. Suddenly, they start questioning your ideas, undermining your contributions, and making snide comments in front of the boss. It's a classic move—the retaliation game at its finest. It's about making sure you know your place in the hierarchy, and if you dare step out of line, there will be consequences.

But here's the kicker: retaliation can be a slow burn. It's not always about grand gestures of vengeance. Sometimes it's the small, seemingly insignificant acts—like being left off an important email thread, your ideas being credited to someone else, or your performance reviews mysteriously lacking any mention of your contributions. These actions are meant to make you question yourself and your value in the company, all while the retaliator gets away with it under the radar.

NOW, HOW DO YOU COMBAT this covert war? First, recognize it for what it is. Retaliation thrives in ambiguity and silence. If you've noticed a pattern where someone starts treating you differently after you speak up or make a suggestion, don't ignore it. Trust your instincts—there's a good chance you're dealing with retaliation.

Next, document everything. When you're on the receiving end of these subtle attacks, keep a record of emails, conversations, and actions that seem off. A paper trail can be your best defense. When things start to get uncomfortable, and you're starting to feel like your work environment is becoming toxic, these documents can help you present a clear case if you need to escalate things to HR.

Then, address it head-on. If the retaliation is coming from a colleague, don't engage in the same petty behavior. Instead, approach them calmly and directly. "I've noticed some tension since our meeting last week, and I wanted to clear the air. If I've said anything that upset you, let's talk it through." This approach shows maturity and confidence, and it puts the ball in their court to either own up to their actions or keep pretending nothing is wrong.

Finally, stay professional. The temptation to retaliate in kind can be overwhelming, but don't do it. Rising above the petty squabbles and continuing to perform at your best will not only make you look better in front of others, but it will also make you feel more in control of the situation. Keep your focus on your work, maintain your integrity, and don't let anyone else drag you down to their level.

IN THE END, THE RETALIATION game is one you can win with patience, professionalism, and the ability to keep your cool under pressure. By recognizing the signs, documenting your interactions, and addressing the issue directly, you'll not only survive the office warzone—you'll emerge as the one with the upper hand.

Chapter 3: The Invisible Wall—When You're Ignored, Not Excluded

Let's talk about the most insidious form of workplace warfare: being ignored. Not outright excluded, like you're the office pariah, but subtly overlooked, dismissed, and excluded from important decisions without anyone actually saying, "You're not invited." Welcome to the land of the Invisible Wall—where you're physically present but mentally and professionally left out.

Imagine this: You've spent weeks crafting a report. You've gone above and beyond, and you're ready to present your findings. The meeting arrives, and as soon as the conversation starts, everyone turns to your colleague Dave from Sales, completely ignoring the fact that you were the one who did all the legwork. Instead of your work being acknowledged, Dave's pulling up a slide deck he didn't even help create. It's like you don't even exist in the room. Welcome to the world of being invisible.

This form of passive exclusion is the favorite weapon of the office's elite—those who can pull the strings without anyone noticing. Maybe it's your manager who always seems to forget to loop you in on important updates or decisions. Maybe it's your colleagues who gather for lunch, but the invite somehow never lands in your inbox. You're there, you're ready, and yet—*nothing*. Your ideas are ignored in meetings, your emails get lost in the shuffle, and somehow, when the decisions are made, you're left out of the loop.

Here's another example: There's a big project deadline coming up, and you're ready to pitch in. But every time you ask if you can help or offer your expertise, you get the same vague responses. "We've got it covered," or "We'll reach out if we need anything," leaving you sitting at your desk, feeling like you're standing outside the door, desperately knocking but never getting in. What's worse? You're still expected to be a team player while others parade their work to the higher-ups as if you don't even exist.

SO, WHAT DO YOU DO? How do you break through that invisible wall?

First, get loud, but not obnoxious. If your contributions are being overlooked, speak up—professionally, of course. In meetings, don't wait to be noticed. If your ideas are being ignored, gently but firmly bring them back into the conversation. For example, "I'd like to circle back to the point I mentioned earlier. It's critical to the direction we're taking." You're not begging for attention, but you are claiming it in a respectful way.

Next, get visible in other ways. Sometimes, you need to take your work elsewhere. If you're not being invited to the important discussions, make sure your work is seen elsewhere. Share your accomplishments in a digestible way—send regular updates to your boss, ask for one-on-one meetings to discuss your contributions, or even suggest putting your work on the team's radar in some form of a presentation. The goal is to make sure that your effort doesn't go unnoticed by people who matter.

Also, establish your value early and often. If you're constantly being overlooked, it may be because you haven't positioned yourself as an essential part of the team. Step up at the beginning of every project. Make it clear where your strengths lie. Don't wait for others to assign you the "big task"—raise your hand, volunteer, and make sure people know what you can bring to the table.

Lastly, don't take it personally. This is a tough one, but it's necessary. Often, being ignored is more about others' shortcomings than about your own. Office dynamics can be awkward and disjointed. People can be busy, distracted, or focused on their own projects. If you let yourself get wrapped up in feeling ignored, you risk internalizing it and letting it affect your performance. Keep your focus on the work and your own growth, regardless of the invisible wall around you.

IN THE WORLD OF OFFICE warfare, being ignored is one of the stealthiest battles you'll face. But armed with the right strategies—speaking up, staying visible, establishing value, and keeping your cool—you can break through that wall and make sure your presence is felt in every room.

Chapter 4: The Perfectionist Pitfall—When Good Enough is Never Enough

There's a special kind of pain that comes with working alongside a perfectionist. You know the type—the ones who hold every project to an impossibly high standard, only to revise it, tweak it, and overanalyze every tiny detail until the work is either delayed or never finished. The problem isn't just the standards they set for themselves—it's the burden they place on everyone else, making you feel like you're stuck in an endless loop of "fixing" things that were fine in the first place.

Here's a classic scenario: You've been assigned a project with a deadline, and you submit your work early, feeling pretty good about it. But then, your perfectionist colleague, let's call her Rachel from Legal, swoops in. She insists that the formatting is slightly off, the font isn't "professional enough," and the wording needs to be changed just a little more to sound "polished." A few tweaks later, you send it back, only to hear from her again—now she wants to rewrite the entire section because she's "not sure it's perfect." You can already feel the deadline slipping away. What started as a solid piece of work is now caught in a perpetual cycle of minor corrections. Welcome to the Perfectionist Pitfall.

But the impact isn't just limited to the perfectionist themselves. When you're working with someone who cannot accept anything less than absolute flawlessness, everything slows down. It's a productivity killer. Team projects get delayed, opportunities for creativity are squashed, and people start to feel like their work is never good enough—no matter how hard they try.

Let's say you're part of a team tasked with putting together a quarterly report. You've done your part, crunched the numbers, and created a draft. You hand it off to Tom, your team lead, who insists on going over every number again—even though you've double-checked them. "Just to be sure," he says. Two days later, he asks you to change the wording of every bullet point, just to "fine-tune" it. By the time the report is ready, the deadline has passed, and everyone is burnt out from the endless edits. This is the Perfectionist Pitfall at work.

SO, HOW DO YOU SURVIVE the perfectionist in the office and break free from this cycle of endless revisions? Here's how:

First, set clear boundaries. If your perfectionist colleague keeps nitpicking your work, set limits early. Politely but firmly explain that you've already reviewed everything and you're confident in its quality. For example: "I've double-checked the numbers and the content. I'm happy to make changes if absolutely necessary, but at this point, I'd like to move forward with the draft we have."

Next, focus on progress, not perfection. Perfectionism is about chasing an unattainable ideal, and it often leads to stagnation. Encourage your team to adopt the "good enough" mindset. Challenge the belief that every detail must be flawless and remind everyone that completing a project is more important than making it perfect. It's not about ignoring quality, but about recognizing when the work is ready to be done.

Also, find ways to collaborate with your perfectionist colleagues rather than being dragged into a series of revisions. When they bring up yet another tweak, respond by asking, "What's the impact of this change? Will it make a significant difference?" This helps reframe the conversation and keeps things moving forward. You can also suggest reviewing the work at specific stages to prevent endless back-and-forth.

Finally, embrace mistakes. Understand that no one is perfect. Mistakes will happen, and that's okay. If something does go wrong, own it, fix it, and learn from it. By demonstrating this mindset, you encourage others to let go of their need for perfection and focus on progress and learning.

THE PERFECTIONIST PITFALL can turn a high-functioning team into a group of stressed-out individuals, trapped in a cycle of revisions and delays. But by setting boundaries, prioritizing progress over perfection, and shifting the focus to collaboration, you can help everyone escape the never-ending pursuit of flawless work and get things done on time—without sacrificing quality or sanity.

Chapter 5: The Micromanager Menace—When Control Take Over

If you've ever been supervised by a micromanager, you know it's like being trapped in a never-ending loop of unnecessary oversight. Every email you send is read and re-read. Every report you produce is scrutinized to the point of absurdity. You get endless feedback on how to "improve" work that's already perfect, and you start questioning your own abilities because your boss seems convinced that you can't do anything without their input. Welcome to the world of the Micromanager Menace, where trust is scarce, and independence is a distant memory.

Micromanagers thrive on control. They are the kind of people who believe that if they aren't involved in every step of a process, it's doomed to fail. They hover over you like a hawk, watching your every move and often giving unsolicited advice or instructions at the most inconvenient times. Picture this: you're deep into a project, and just as you think you're making progress, your boss sends an email asking for a detailed breakdown of your tasks, every hour of your day, and every person you've spoken to. It's as though they don't believe you can handle the job without constant supervision.

The problem is, micromanagement creates a toxic work environment. Team members become resentful, stressed, and disengaged. They feel like their expertise and autonomy aren't trusted, which leads to frustration. As the micromanager continues to hover, employees' confidence erodes, and creativity takes a backseat. You can't be innovative when someone's looking over your shoulder every minute, making sure you're following their exact instructions. In the end, micromanagement leads to decreased productivity, burnout, and high employee turnover.

Let's take Sarah from HR as an example. She's running a recruitment campaign and has everything lined up. The job descriptions are polished, the strategy is clear, and she's ready to move forward. But then, her manager swoops in, giving feedback on every little detail: "Can you change this phrase?" "This sentence doesn't sound quite right." "Let's tweak the format here." By the time Sarah is done implementing all the changes, the deadline has passed, and the campaign has been delayed. What should have been a smooth process is now bogged down by unnecessary revisions.

SO, HOW DO YOU DEAL with the Micromanager Menace and reclaim your autonomy?

First, set clear expectations. Micromanagers often lack trust in their team's abilities. So, it's essential to be proactive in demonstrating your competence. At the start of a project, outline clear goals, deliverables, and timelines. This gives your manager confidence that you've got things under control, and it reduces the need for constant check-ins. Make it clear that you'll update them at key milestones, but don't need continuous oversight.

Second, practice assertive communication. When your micromanager starts to overstep, assert yourself respectfully. Politely tell them when you don't need additional input. For example, "I appreciate your feedback, but I'm confident the direction I'm taking is the right one. I'll keep you updated on any major changes." This shows them you're in control without being confrontational.

Third, manage their expectations with regular updates. If your manager feels the need to oversee everything, take the initiative and give regular updates before they ask for them. This can be a weekly summary of progress or a daily brief to show what's been accomplished. By keeping them in the loop, you can reduce the number of times they feel the need to intervene.

Fourth, create a feedback loop. Sometimes, micromanagers fear failure and feel they need to control everything to prevent mistakes. Encourage a feedback loop that involves giving them a chance to review progress at certain milestones, rather than all the time. You can say, "I'm going to work on this next part, and I'd love your feedback by Friday if you have any concerns." This establishes clear times for input without constant interference.

Finally, empower your team. If you're in a leadership position, avoid micromanaging your team. Empower them by delegating tasks, setting clear expectations, and trusting them to get the job done. Not only will this improve your team's morale, but it will also free you from the cycle of feeling like you need to be involved in every tiny detail.

THE MICROMANAGER MENACE may seem like an unstoppable force, but with clear communication, setting boundaries, and building trust, you can minimize its impact and regain the freedom to work without being constantly micromanaged. It's time to take back your autonomy and make work, well, work again.

Chapter 6: The Procrastination Nation—When Deadlines Aren't Deadlines

Procrastination—the fine art of putting things off until the very last minute, and then panicking about it. We've all been there, whether it's the pressure of too many tasks, the fear of failure, or the simple joy of avoiding work. But when procrastination becomes a culture in the office, it's a different ball game entirely. Welcome to Procrastination Nation, where deadlines are mere suggestions, and "I'll do it later" is a national motto.

Picture this: you're working on a project that's due in a week. You know it's coming up, but somehow, the urgency doesn't hit until the night before. You've spent the past few days scrolling through social media, chatting with coworkers about irrelevant things, and staring blankly at your screen. Suddenly, the clock is ticking, and you're racing against time. The stress levels are through the roof. You can't focus because your brain is doing gymnastics to avoid the inevitable. Sound familiar?

But procrastination isn't just about avoiding one task—it's the ripple effect it has across the office. Take Tim, for example. He has an important report due by Friday, but he's been putting it off all week. By Wednesday, his manager asks for an update, and Tim, in a panic, promises to have it done by the end of the day. Fast forward to Friday, and Tim is still scrambling, sending out a report that's rushed, incomplete, and full of errors. Not only does this affect Tim's credibility, but it also delays the entire team's work. His procrastination impacts everyone.

The Procrastination Nation problem grows when it's a team issue. If everyone is procrastinating, you'll find your projects stuck in limbo, deadlines missed, and the quality of work suffering. Everyone starts blaming the system, the workload, or the lack of resources, but at the end of the day, it's the procrastination mindset that's holding everyone back. It's a collective drag on productivity.

SO, HOW DO YOU TACKLE the Procrastination Nation and break free from the grip of delay?

First, break it down into manageable chunks. One of the main reasons people procrastinate is because the task feels too overwhelming. Instead of looking at the massive report that's due in two weeks, break it down into smaller tasks. "Today, I'll work on the introduction," or "I'll finish the data analysis first." When you focus on one piece at a time, the task feels less daunting, and you're more likely to get started.

Second, create hard deadlines for yourself. Even though the official deadline may be weeks away, create mini-deadlines for yourself along the way. Set a deadline for completing the research, another for drafting the document, and so on. When you break up your project into smaller deadlines, it's easier to hold yourself accountable, and the pressure to perform feels more manageable.

Third, remove distractions. If you know that you procrastinate because of social media, chatting with coworkers, or constant notifications, take proactive steps to minimize distractions. Turn off your phone's notifications, use apps that block distracting websites, or even move to a quieter area of the office. By eliminating distractions, you'll reduce the temptation to delay the work.

Fourth, make a public commitment. Telling someone about your goals or setting up an accountability partner can be a game-changer. If you know your coworker is going to ask for progress updates, you're more likely to stay on track. You could even start a group chat where everyone shares their goals and deadlines—if you know you're reporting progress, you'll be more motivated to follow through.

Finally, reward yourself for progress. After completing a task, reward yourself in some way—take a break, grab a coffee, or spend a few minutes doing something you enjoy. Positive reinforcement makes it easier to keep going, and helps you associate progress with something enjoyable.

PROCRASTINATION NATION isn't a lost cause. By breaking tasks into smaller chunks, setting deadlines, eliminating distractions, making commitments, and rewarding yourself, you can escape the cycle of delay and get back on track. Time to stop putting things off—your future self will thank you.

Chapter 7: The Blame Game—When Everything Goes Wrong, But No One's At Fault

Shucks! It's the Blame Game—the classic office pastime. It's that special sport where everyone's pointing fingers, but no one's taking responsibility. This toxic little game becomes especially rampant when things go wrong—projects fail, deadlines are missed, and clients get upset. But instead of taking accountability, people scramble to shift the responsibility onto others. It's not their fault the project failed. It's the team member who missed the meeting, the manager who didn't give enough direction, or the system that was too complicated.

Let's take a look at how this plays out in a typical office. Sarah is leading a team to launch a new marketing campaign. The campaign is behind schedule because the design team delayed their deliverables by two weeks. Now, with the deadline looming, Sarah is running around, telling everyone that the marketing plan is in jeopardy because the design team couldn't meet their deadlines. Meanwhile, the design team is blaming Sarah for not providing clearer instructions and not having a realistic timeline.

The irony? No one is taking responsibility for their part in the process. The marketing team is angry at design, design is frustrated with marketing, and both teams are secretly blaming senior leadership for not setting the right expectations. No one is saying, "Okay, maybe I could have done things differently," and the result is a culture of finger-pointing and resentment.

THE ART OF OFFICE COMBAT: CONQUER YOUR WORKPLACE, ONE DISASTER AT A TIME

The Blame Game isn't just frustrating—it actively destroys productivity. Instead of focusing on solutions, everyone is busy casting blame. This constant deflection not only damages trust between teams but also creates a sense of helplessness. If everyone's blaming everyone else, nothing ever gets done.

SO, HOW DO YOU BREAK the Blame Game cycle and create a culture of accountability?

First, take ownership. It starts with you. When things go wrong, resist the urge to point fingers. Instead, ask yourself, "What could I have done differently?" Acknowledge your part in the situation and be open about it. Saying, "I should've communicated better with the team," or "I didn't manage my time as well as I should have" sets a positive example and encourages others to do the same. Taking ownership of your actions—even when the situation is tough—builds trust and shows that you're committed to improving.

Second, foster open communication. Often, the Blame Game stems from poor communication. People don't speak up early enough when issues arise, and then they scramble to shift blame when the problem snowballs. Encourage open dialogue within your team. If there's an issue, bring it up immediately, and talk about what can be done to solve it. Be proactive about identifying potential problems and offer solutions instead of waiting for someone else to take the fall.

Third, hold people accountable without blaming. Holding team members accountable doesn't mean calling them out in front of others or assigning blame. It means addressing the issue directly and focusing on how to fix it. For example, if a team member missed a deadline, instead of blaming them, you can say, "This delay is impacting our project timeline. How can we adjust to get back on track?" The focus is on solutions, not fault.

Fourth, shift the focus to collaboration. Encourage a culture where people work together to solve problems rather than looking for someone to blame. When a project goes off track, the response should be, "What can we do to make this right?" This collaborative mindset fosters a sense of teamwork and shared responsibility. By focusing on fixing the issue instead of finding who's to blame, you not only address the problem faster but also strengthen the overall team dynamic.

Lastly, celebrate successes together. When things go right, share the credit. Don't let success be an individual achievement. Acknowledge everyone who contributed, and make it clear that you achieved the goal together. This reinforces the idea that everyone is in it together—successes and failures alike.

THE BLAME GAME IS A productivity killer. By fostering a culture of ownership, open communication, accountability, and collaboration, you can break the cycle of blame and create a more effective and positive work environment. It's time to stop pointing fingers and start solving problems.

Chapter 8: The Incompetence Epidemic—When Everyone's Too Busy to Do Their Job Properly

Incompetence—the silent killer of productivity, efficiency, and office morale. It's a pandemic that spreads quietly but swiftly, infecting every corner of an organization. The problem with incompetence is that it often masquerades as something else: "lack of experience," "insufficient training," or even "miscommunication." But at its core, it's the failure to perform at the expected level. It's when people aren't doing their jobs properly, and it's everyone else who ends up picking up the slack.

Let's break it down. Imagine you're working on a critical project that involves a multi-step process. You've been assigned to handle the final report, and everything is going fine—until you realize that your colleague, Dave, has misinterpreted the data. Not only that, but he's handed over a report that doesn't align with the project's goals. You're now left scrambling to redo the work. The problem? Dave doesn't seem to notice that the report is flawed. He's too busy chatting with the office admin about his weekend plans to even double-check his work.

Or take Sandra, who's supposed to be managing the client communications for a new account. Instead of addressing client concerns with clarity, she's sending vague emails that leave the client more confused than ever. When you bring it up, she brushes it off and says, "I thought they'd get it." Her inability to do her job properly is not only annoying—it's damaging the relationship with the client and risking the business.

But incompetence isn't always as glaring as the examples above. Sometimes, it's the subtle things: the team member who constantly forgets to meet deadlines, the manager who can't keep track of the team's progress, or the colleague who consistently drops the ball on small tasks that pile up. The real issue here is not that people are intentionally lazy, but that their lack of competence affects everyone else's ability to do their job well. It creates frustration, stress, and ultimately, a toxic workplace culture.

SO HOW DO WE TACKLE incompetence in the office? Simple—by addressing it directly, with a mix of clear expectations, support, and accountability.

First, set clear expectations. One of the primary causes of incompetence is that people don't know what's expected of them. If you don't clearly define roles, goals, and benchmarks, people won't know how to meet them. Whether it's a detailed job description, clear instructions for a project, or a timeline for completion, make sure everyone knows exactly what is expected. This reduces confusion and sets people up for success.

Second, invest in training and development. Incompetence often comes from a lack of knowledge or skills. It's easy to assume that people should just "know" how to do things, but in reality, not everyone comes equipped with the same expertise. Provide opportunities for your team to improve their skills. Whether through formal training, mentoring, or self-paced learning, give people the tools they need to perform their job competently.

Third, offer regular feedback. If someone is consistently underperforming, don't wait until it's too late to address it. Provide constructive feedback early on. Be specific about what they're doing wrong and offer guidance on how to improve. Instead of focusing on the failure, focus on the solution. Feedback should be a continuous process, not just a once-a-year performance review.

Fourth, hold people accountable. Incompetence thrives when there are no consequences for poor performance. If someone isn't doing their job properly, hold them accountable. Set performance benchmarks and be consistent in enforcing them. If someone is struggling, work with them to improve, but make it clear that consistent incompetence will have real consequences. It's not about punishing people, but about maintaining the standards that drive success.

Finally, cultivate a culture of excellence. This doesn't mean everyone has to be perfect all the time. But when you foster an environment that values competence, attention to detail, and accountability, people are more likely to step up and perform at their best. Celebrate small wins, acknowledge improvements, and encourage a sense of pride in one's work. When people feel motivated and supported, their competency will naturally rise.

INCOMPETENCE CAN DESTROY an office, but it doesn't have to. By setting clear expectations, investing in training, offering feedback, holding people accountable, and creating a culture of excellence, you can reduce the impact of incompetence and foster a high-performing, efficient workplace. It's time to raise the bar—and make incompetence a thing of the past.

Conclusion: The Battle's Not Over—It's Time to Rise Up!

Congratulations, brave office warriors! You've made it through the trenches of gossip, incompetence, the blame game, and all the other toxic pitfalls that have threatened to sabotage your career and morale. But here's the thing: your battle isn't over. In fact, it's only just begun.

You're armed with knowledge. You've got the tools to fight back, whether it's through taking ownership, creating clear expectations, or building a culture of accountability. You've learned how to push through the chaos and emerge victorious. Now, it's time to put everything into action.

But here's your challenge: don't be complacent. Don't sit back and wait for someone else to fix things. The change starts with you. Every email you send, every meeting you lead, every conversation you have can be a victory for the good guys. You are the ones who set the tone, who refuse to let mediocrity win, who rise above the drama and create a workplace culture that values productivity, accountability, and respect.

THE OFFICE WORLD ISN'T going to change overnight. But if you want to build something great, you have to be willing to put in the work and challenge the status quo. Embrace your role as the office warrior—your mission is to fight the battles of incompetence, poor communication, and lackluster leadership, and to do so with strategy, humor, and grit. Don't wait for permission to make a difference. Lead by example. Speak up when you see problems, and stand tall when others are too scared to act. Your team needs a hero. Be that hero.

Remember, the goal is simple: to build an office where people are competent, accountable, and actually enjoy working together. Where the drama is minimal, the productivity is high, and everyone can leave the office feeling like they did something worth doing.

So, what are you waiting for? Grab your armor, rally your team, and let's win this war—one email at a time, one meeting at a time, one conversation at a time. The battlefield may be messy, but with the right mindset, you'll conquer it.

And before you march off into battle, here's a joke to keep the mood light:

Why don't skeletons ever fight each other at work?

Because they don't have the guts.

Now, go make a difference!

THE END

About the Author

Marako Marcus is a consultant, coach, and public speaker with a reputation for being straight to the point—no fluff, no excuses. He helps executives, teams, and individuals face their challenges head-on, cutting through the corporate nonsense and delivering results that matter. With years of experience working with organizations of all sizes, Marako knows exactly what's wrong with most workplaces and how to fix them—without the usual corporate jargon.

A master of tough love and tough conversations, he's a coach who tells it like it is and makes sure you know exactly where you stand. His approach is simple: if you're not getting it done, stop whining and start acting. He's worked with leaders who need a wake-up call and teams who need someone to light a fire under them.

When he's not stirring up success in the business world, Marako unleashes his creativity as a musician. Yes, he's the guy who can juggle spreadsheets and compose a killer track at the same time—proving that sharp focus can strike the right chord in both the boardroom and the studio. Marako's blend of directness and creativity makes him a unique voice in the business world—and someone you'll want to listen to.

BOOK LINKS AVAILABLE at https://linktr.ee/marakomarcusbooks

www.ingramcontent.com/pod-product-compliance
Lightning Source LLC
Chambersburg PA
CBHW070944220526
45469CB00007B/2511